Samo Kreutz

The Stars for Tonight

Cyberwit.net
HIG 45 Kaushambi Kunj, Kalindipuram
Allahabad - 211011 (U.P.) India
http://www.cyberwit.net
Tel: +(91) 9415091004
E-mail: info@cyberwit.net

Printed in India.

grandad's car
in my childhood memories
brighter than the stars

Me and the wind

*e*arly morning
courier service van
carries the dawn

*s*veže nastal svit
kombi kurirske službe
prevaža zoro

*f*irst glance
a softener awakens
the smell of flowers

gentle light
already blooming
the bird sounds

raising the blinds
with me in the bedroom
everyday rumble

early glow
listening to baby babbling
a scent of the flowers

*u*nderwear
the sunshine beside it
completely undressed

*t*he Holy Forty
among the thorns
an image of a man

*b*almy breeze
severely emaciated
a snowman

*m*arch equinox
I open the doors wide
to show the winter out

*e*vergreen
entering my room
more and more sun

*s*pring breath
at my fingertips
a toddler's crying

lengthening days
less and less time
for boredom

tree under the lamp
its just burst bud
lit with gold

small estate
a path toward the field
full of sunshine

granny's garden
already sowed in it
the fragrances

*a*pril sun
my black and white photo
rich in the colours

*p*ostman's arrival
faster at him than I am
a small sparrow

bird sounds
chainsaw rumble
silenced

screaming child
his comrade in the game
a spongy birch stump

linden tree
lightly touching buds
my runaway thoughts

*m*ay haze
a boy's whisper to his mum
attracts the sun

*c*ouple in love
inside them both
a perfect haiku

*h*orseman statue
above his sooty head
wreath of white clouds

*f*riend's secret
the first to know it
me and the wind

*h*omeless
wandering through the city
the magnolia scent

*y*elping dog
rubbish in the breeze
such a terrible enemy

lazy drizzle
in a small trash can
a big flood

raindrop in my palm
severely prolonged
the life line

granite cube
its sharp edges
greened

*s*towaway
traveling in my nose
an elder tree scent

*c*ity model
bigger than a house
the ordinary fly

*l*ibrary visit
among a pile of books
I find a boy's laughter

people at the shop
with them in the queue
blooming tree shadows

bus stop
waiting for a lift
the forsythia scent

family in the car
riding together with it
sun and the cloud

*b*onfire
starting to melt
my years

*s*pacious motorhome
at the table with people
trees and the moon

*p*rostran avtodom
skupaj za mizo z ljudmi
drevje ter mesec

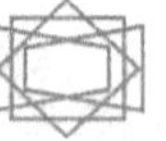

A pinch of sunshine

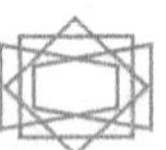

children tricycle
going to the world
a toddler and a dawn

kolesarnica
ob otroškem triciklu
odhaja zor v svet

light morning breeze
knocking at my doors
a bird singing

summer sunrise
almost stuck to mine
a little boy's shadow

the alley
waiting for its owner
scent of a perfume

cleaned up quarter
bush without any rubbish
just boring

crowded market
the biggest attraction
a baby in a pram

strolling children
far ahead of them
their lively voices

everyday bustle
going the same way
me and a boy's laughter

linden tree in bloom
a nearby shrubs adorns
with its scent

sea of greenery
hidden from everywhere
the graveyard

juicy curses
the sound of bird chirping
greatly drowned out

Ljubljanica riverbank
walking with the tourists
a bitter crying

safety mask
totally hidden
the crab

flea market
louder than huckster
a nearby crow

city park
the liveliest in the game
granny and her grandson

wedding ceremony
without any invitation
summer breeze

sunny afternoon
my neighbour greets
me a little warmer

*h*idden lake
I have a rendezvous
with tranquillity

*h*unting tower
a bird from it observes
me in the clearing

*f*orest glade
with strawberries ripens
a pinch of sunshine

*s*evere heat
a young tree wrapped
into the strip of my shadow

*m*ushroom season
looking for chanterelles
I find the sunshine

*m*uddy rut
clearer as the real one
rainbow in the puddle

love without borders
stuck to the daisy
a big snail

the longest day
thinner and thinner
our shadows

low trampoline
much higher than the sun
a boy in jump

*al*most dusk
late at work with me
linden tree fragrance

my youthful photo
as I look in the mirror
only eyes the same

*h*ot evening
drinking from a puddle
the flower shadow

moon in veils
a pale streetlamp
shines for them both

village well   vaški studenec
a brown birch leaf sinks   rjavkast list breze tone
under the weight of a star   pod težo zvezde

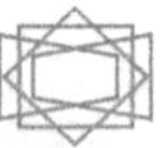

Tree shadows

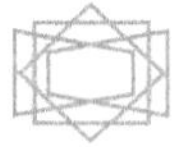

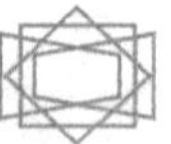

*t*rain station —
among a pile of luggage
dawn light

*p*ostanek vlaka
med kopico prtljage
odhajajoč svit

*a*utumn daybreak
looking for their sun
a procession of elderly

*s*cared baby
in his little world
too many adults

*k*itchen table
at the master's place
a tiny spider

*t*ablecloth
the quality of embroidery
inspects the fly

*u*nsweetened tea
tasting a little bitter
rainbow in it

*a*lley cat
in her messy hair
first traces of sun

*t*earful boy
newcomer carries away
the unstoppable crying

old woman among toddlers
even more noticeable
her limping

wrinkled palm
touches it gently
a small fly

fresh frost
glowing in a new colour
a broken bench

café noise
a crow at the entrance
the loudest guest

tinny bird
my shadow's touch
too much for him

fox den
howling voice in it
just strong breeze

curved dandelion
heavy load on the stem
an oak's shadow

huge house
not high enough to stop
a leaf in the wind

gale
blown away
my tiredness

low cloudiness
house without the roof
no longer uncovered

heavy drops
discarded chair
all broken

end of the storm
wet trees are exhaling
the rainbow

*d*og on the leash
his reflection in the pool
entirely free

*b*ird footprints
two distant puddles
no longer separated

*t*he fallen tree
even completely dead
an obstacle to the river

*d*ug up potatoes
at the farmer in the field
a multitude of suns

*s*trenuous walk
on my shoulders
tree shadows

*m*assive oak
covered with one leaf
a plane in the sky

*f*lock of goats
late autumn breeze
their herdsman

*d*og among the sheeps
full of loudly barking
faraway woods

*g*olden glow in the crown
by the naked tree
a slim sunflower

*s*hadowy path
bearing a large house
an ant

*s*mell of food
under a skyscraper
voice of a hungry kitten

*g*arbage man
on his rusty shovel
leaves and the sun

*c*oming home
I dandle in my lap
the late afternoon

*w*ater trough
gathered around it
the house shadows

a faint bell echo
the noisy truck takes it
out of the village

*w*ire fence
slim tree shadows
unstoppable

*s*ound of a siren
only a sparrow
alarmed

*m*ovement restriction
on my home doormat
inscription *welcome*

closed border
crosses it freely
only wind

evening forest
not quite big enough
for all the shadows

huge barn
calmly resting on a hay
the moonlight

*c*old night breeze
dressed in a girl's jacket
a stone pillar

*c*louds everywhere   *p*ovsod oblaki
shining streetlamps   odsevi cestnih svetilk
stars for tonight   zvezde za to noč

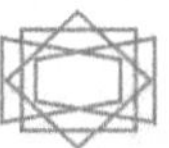

Embracing the stars

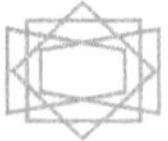

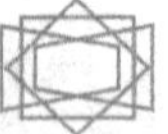

*d*arkness outside
school in a small shack
so full of brightness

*t*emina zunaj
za okni stare šole
razkošje luči

*o*ld woman
in her cup on the table
tea and morning silence

winter dawn
chirping instead of birds
voice from the radio

clock tick-tack
no more place in my room
even for a whisper

melting ice
all the vehicles
iridescent

village street
coming and going
the morning wind

light rain
hiding in my bed
today's daylight

leafless tree
pale winter sun
his aura

cross in the village
Christ and the mist
share it in unity

rumble of a chainsaw
the fog around it
cut to pieces

outdoor table
wiping off dust
tree branch shadow

shop window
today's special offer
a rainbow

noticeboard
under a layer of ice
the woman in swimsuit

mansion poster
on a bench beneath
only void

*m*orning tiredness
using castle funicular
my gaze

*p*ublic park
with me on a walk
everyday problems

*w*inter frost
bent grasses
all the same

curved hayrack
hanging on splines
only shadows

large flyer
the snowman gazes
at a half-dressed woman

stooped man
too heavy to bear
a frozen raindrop

*n*oisy drunkard
not scared at all
a nearby bird

*h*omeless man
between him and the others
double social distance

*s*now on the fingers
slightly less empty
a beggar's palm

branchy bush
trace of greenery in it
the face mask

quarantine
running away from his house
footprints in the snow

I overtake an old man
his stomping walks
alongside with me

wintry afternoon
words coming out of my mouth –
even they are white

burning Advent candle
banished into the corner
all the shadows

lollipop
one more time
I become a child

*f*ather's crutches
leaning on them
the whole house

*ch*aos in the room
lost between the clutter
a beam of the moon

*g*randparents' home
sitting alone in the chair
a memory

*m*embrane of ice
underneath a last year's leaf
well preserved

*s*outh wind
not quite himself
a snow angel

*s*helter
teaching me how to hope
a homeless dog

late evening murk
illuminating the path
the sun in my minds

macadam road
embracing the stars
only dust

Valentine's night
keeping me awake
the sounds of cat's love

*m*eeting with the girlfriend
unusually upright
his posture

*y*oung sweethearts
deeply in their shadow
an elderly couple

*t*races in the snow
strolling with me
new beginnings

*p*ublic lighting
walking through the city
me and my split shadow

*s*nowy path
I pause to inhale
the tranquillity

zasnežena pot
nebrzdano vdihujem
spokojnost sveta

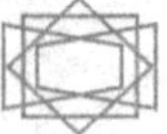

A WORD OR TWO ABOUT THE AUTHOR

Samo Kreutz lives in Ljubljana, Slovenia. He began to write as an eight-year-old boy, when he wrote his first story (and later a poem). One day his parents told him that simply by writing he cannot earn enough for a decent life, so he replied that he will become a writer and a joiner. Now, at the age of forty-five, he is not yet a joiner (nor a carpenter), but the Bachelor of Economics, who besides poetry and short stories, also writes novels and haiku (since 2011). He is the author of nine books (three of them are haiku books), all published by the Ekslibris, publishing house in Ljubljana. His work has appeared in various Slovenian literary magazines, anthologies, on national Radio, and on several international websites (e- and printed journals).

A NOTE ABOUT THE BOOK

The Stars for Tonight consists of 155 haiku. They can be found (in English, Slovene or both versions) in printed journals: *Akitsu Quarterly, Seashores: Haiku Journal,* and *Taj Mahal Review,* on websites: *Akita International Haiku Network, Asahi Haikuist Network, Autumn Moon Haiku Journal, Chrysanthemum, Cold Moon Journal, Creatrix Haiku and Poetry Journal, Dwelling Literary, First Literary Review- East, Frameless Sky: Art Video Journal, Haiku Commentary, Ink Sweat & Tears: The poetry and prose webzine, Jalmurra: Art and Poetry Journal, Locutio, Poetry Pea, Quatrain.Fish Zine, Stardust Haiku Online Journal, Under the Basho,* and *Wales Haiku Journal,* in anthologies: *Haiku zbornik: Ludbreg, Pesem si: zbornik, Samoborski haiku susreti Darko Plažanin,* and in quite a few broadcasts on the national Radio.

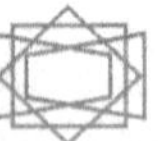

CONTENTS

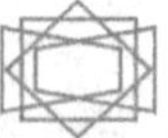